St. Mary's High School

THE MAKING OF THE MODERN WORLD

1945 TO THE PRESENT

Trade, Economic Life, and Globalization

BOOKS IN THE SERIES

Culture and Customs in a Connected World

Education, Poverty, and Inequality

Food, Population, and the Environment

Governance and the Quest for Security

Health and Medicine

Migration and Refugees

Science and Technology

Trade, Economic Life, and Globalization

Women, Minorities, and Changing Social Structures

THE MAKING OF THE MODERN WORLD

1945 TO THE PRESENT

Trade, Economic Life, and Globalization

John Perritano

SERIES ADVISOR
Ruud van Dijk

Mason Crest

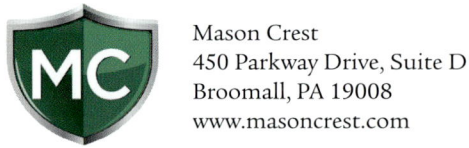

Mason Crest
450 Parkway Drive, Suite D
Broomall, PA 19008
www.masoncrest.com

© 2017 by Mason Crest, an imprint of National Highlights, Inc. All rights reserved. No part of this publication may be reproduced or transmitted in any form or by any means, electronic or mechanical, including photocopying, recording, taping, or any information storage and retrieval system, without permission from the publisher.

Produced and developed by MTM Publishing.
www.mtmpublishing.com

President and Project Coordinator: Valerie Tomaselli
Designer: Sherry Williams, Oxygen Design Group
Copyeditor: Lee Motteler, GeoMap Corp.
Editorial Coordinator: Andrea St. Aubin
Proofreader: Peter Jaskowiak

ISBN: 978-1-4222-3642-0
Series ISBN: 978-1-4222-3634-5
Ebook ISBN: 978-1-4222-8286-1

Library of Congress Cataloging-in-Publication Data
On file

Printed and bound in the United States of America.

First printing
9 8 7 6 5 4 3 2 1

QR CODES AND LINKS TO THIRD PARTY CONTENT
You may gain access to certain third party content ("Third Party Sites") by scanning and using the QR Codes that appear in this publication (the "QR Codes"). We do not operate or control in any respect any information, products or services on such Third Party Sites linked to by us via the QR Codes included in this publication, and we assume no responsibility for any materials you may access using the QR Codes. Your use of the QR Codes may be subject to terms, limitations, or restrictions set forth in the applicable terms of use or otherwise established by the owners of the Third Party Sites. Our linking to such Third Party Sites via the QR Codes does not imply an endorsement or sponsorship of such Third Party Sites, or the information, products or services offered on or through the Third Party Sites, nor does it imply an endorsement or sponsorship of this publication by the owners of such Third Party Sites.

Contents

Series Introduction 6
CHAPTER 1: A Global Economy 9
CHAPTER 2: Spheres of Influence 17
CHAPTER 3: Consumer Societies Emerge in the West 25
CHAPTER 4: Cold War Wanes, Free Trade Takes Hold 33
CHAPTER 5: Free Markets Rule 41
CHAPTER 6: Globalization in Today's World 49
Timeline 56
Further Research 59
Index 60
Photo Credits 63
About the Author and Advisor 64

KEY ICONS TO LOOK FOR:

Words to understand: These words with their easy-to-understand definitions will increase the reader's understanding of the text while building vocabulary skills.

Sidebars: This boxed material within the main text allows readers to build knowledge, gain insights, explore possibilities, and broaden their perspectives by weaving together additional information to provide realistic and holistic perspectives.

Educational Videos: Readers can view videos by scanning our QR codes, providing them with additional educational content to supplement the text. Examples include news coverage, moments in history, speeches, iconic sports moments and much more!

Text-dependent questions: These questions send the reader back to the text for more careful attention to the evidence presented there.

Research projects: Readers are pointed toward areas of further inquiry connected to each chapter. Suggestions are provided for projects that encourage deeper research and analysis.

Series Introduction

In 1945, at the end of World War II, the world had to start afresh in many ways. The war had affected the entire world, destroying cities, sometimes entire regions, and killing millions. At the end of the war, millions more were displaced or on the move, while hunger, disease, and poverty threatened survivors everywhere the war had been fought.

Politically, the old, European-dominated order had been discredited. Western European democracies had failed to stop Hitler, and in Asia they had been powerless against imperial Japan. The autocratic, militaristic Axis powers had been defeated. But their victory was achieved primarily through the efforts of the Soviet Union—a communist dictatorship—and the United States, which was the only democracy powerful enough to aid Great Britain and the other Allied powers in defeating the Axis onslaught. With the European colonial powers weakened, the populations of their respective empires now demanded their independence.

The war had truly been a global catastrophe. It underlined the extent to which peoples and countries around the world were interconnected and interdependent. However, the search for shared approaches to major, global challenges in the postwar world—symbolized by the founding of the United Nations—was soon overshadowed by the Cold War. The leading powers in this contest, the United States and the Soviet Union, represented mutually exclusive visions for the postwar world. The Soviet Union advocated collectivism, centrally planned economies, and a leading role for the Communist Party. The United States sought to promote liberal democracy, symbolized by free markets and open political systems. Each believed fervently in the promise and justice of its vision for the future. And neither thought it could compromise on what it considered vital interests. Both were concerned about whose influence would dominate Europe, for example, and to whom newly independent nations in the non-Western world would pledge their allegiance. As a result, the postwar world would be far from peaceful.

As the Cold War proceeded, peoples living beyond the Western world and outside the control of the Soviet Union began to find their voices. Driven by decolonization, the developing world, or so-called Third World, took on a new importance. In particular, countries in these areas were potential allies on both sides of the Cold War. As the newly independent peoples established their own identities and built viable states, they resisted the sometimes coercive pull of the Cold War superpowers, while also trying to use them for their own ends. In addition, a new Communist China, established in 1949 and the largest country in the developing world, was deeply entangled within the Cold War contest between communist and capitalist camps. Over the coming decades, however, it would come to act ever more independently from either the United States or the Soviet Union.

During the war, governments had made significant strides in developing new technologies in areas such as aviation, radar, missile technology, and, most ominous, nuclear energy. Scientific and technological breakthroughs achieved in a military context held promise for civilian applications, and thus were poised to contribute to recovery and, ultimately, prosperity. In other fields, it also seemed time for a fresh start. For example, education could be used to "re-educate" members of aggressor nations and further Cold War agendas, but education could also help more people take advantage of, and contribute to, the possibilities of the new age of science and technology.

For several decades after 1945, the Cold War competition seemed to dominate, and indeed define, the postwar world. Driven by ideology, the conflict extended into politics, economics, science and technology, and culture. Geographically, it came to affect virtually the entire world. From our twenty-first-century vantage point, however, it is clear that well before the Cold War's end in the late 1980s, the world had been moving on from the East-West conflict.

Looking back, it appears that, despite divisions—between communist and capitalist camps, or between developed and developing countries—the world after 1945 was growing more and more interconnected. After the Cold War, this increasingly came to be called "globalization." People in many different places faced shared challenges. And as time went on, an awareness of this interconnectedness grew. One response by people in and outside of governments was to seek common approaches, to think and act globally. Another was to protect national, local, or private autonomy, to keep the outside world at bay. Neither usually existed by itself; reality was generally some combination of the two.

Thematically organized, the nine volumes in this series explore how the post–World War II world gradually evolved from the fractured ruins of 1945, through the various crises of the Cold War and the decolonization process, to a world characterized by interconnectedness and interdependence. The accounts in these volumes reinforce each other, and are best studied together. Taking them as a whole will build a broad understanding of the ways in which "globalization" has become the defining feature of the world in the early twenty-first century.

However, the volumes are designed to stand on their own. Tracing the evolution of trade and the global economy, for example, the reader will learn enough about the political context to get a broader understanding of the times. Of course, studying economic developments will likely lead to curiosity about scientific and technological progress, social and cultural change, poverty and education, and more. In other words, studying one volume should lead to interest in the others. In the end, no element of our globalizing world can be fully understood in isolation.

The volumes do not have to be read in a specific order. It is best to be led by one's own interests in deciding where to start. What we recommend is a curious, critical stance throughout the study of the world's history since World War II: to keep asking questions about the causes of events, to keep looking for connections to deepen your understanding of how we have gotten to where we are today. If students achieve this goal with the help of our volumes, we—and they—will have succeeded.

—Ruud van Dijk

The Galesburg Antique Mall, where the last Maytag refrigerator to come off the town's assembly line can be seen.

WORDS TO UNDERSTAND

capitalist: relating to the free-market system based on private ownership of the means of production.

communism: political and economic system in which the state controls the means of production.

devaluation: lowering of the value of a nation's currency.

infrastructure: large-scale public systems and services, such as roads and water supplies.

liberalized: relating to economic competition free from government restraint.

tariffs: duties, or fees, levied by a government on imported or exported goods.

CHAPTER 1

A Global Economy

The refrigerator sits at the Galesburg Antiques Mall in downtown Galesburg, Illinois, collecting dust and stares from customers. It's a nondescript appliance—a white Maytag with the freezer on top. Millions just like it have been sold, and most, one would suspect, are still being used in kitchens around the world.

Yet this refrigerator is different from all the others. In September 2004, the Maytag factory here—where this refrigerator was made—closed and moved its operation to Mexico. The fridge was the last one assembled in this city of 32,000.

As the appliance made its way down the assembly line, employees took a black marker and signed their names to it. A few months after the shuttering, Barack Obama, then running for the U.S. Senate, blamed globalization for the plant's demise and the loss of 1,600 jobs.

Galesburg, once an example of the promise of globalization, had become a reminder that globalization can go horribly wrong. But across the globe, by the time the Maytag plant closed in Galesburg, a massive Taiwan-based manufacturing company, Foxconn, had opened a new factory in Taiyuan, in the Shanxi Province of mainland China. Foxconn would come to expand into several countries, including Brazil and Japan, and would play a major role in producing parts for Apple's iPhone and other consumer electronics. Despite nagging controversies surrounding its treatment of workers, Foxconn and other manufacturers in China have been responsible for lifting huge numbers of Chinese peasants out of poverty and into the middle class.

Given the trade-offs involved in globalization, it's not surprising that support for opening economic borders is qualified, to say the least. Néstor Kirchner, president of Argentina from 2003 to 2007, understood the impact that the bipolarization of globalization can have on people. "We must create a kind of globalization that works for everyone . . . not just for a few," he once said.

Connecting the World

Whether you are putting on a pair of jeans, texting a friend, pumping gas, traveling in a jetliner, or using a computer at school, globalization is at the very heart of your life. Globalization is the way nations use technology, communication, and transportation to connect with each other culturally, politically, and economically.

Globalization makes it easy to buy and sell goods. It fuels trade and affects the way everyone lives. It brings people together and allows businesses to make products more inexpensively. According to many economists, increased trade and economic activity resulting from globalization have created new economic opportunities for many in the developing world, offering a way out of poverty and into the middle class. Yet, according to others, globalization widens the gap between rich and poor and exploits the misuse of natural resources. Some even argue that, as countries interact across borders, it erases old traditions and old jobs in favor of new ways of seeing the world and new ways of working.

War's Aftermath

The modern era of globalization was ushered in after World War II. The war wreaked havoc on the world, killing more than 60 million people (though no one knows the exact number) and destroying the economies of Europe and much of Asia. The United States was the only major power that emerged from the war virtually unscathed and with its economy in robust shape.

Led by President Franklin Roosevelt, and later Harry S. Truman, the United States envisioned a postwar world of **liberalized** free trade and open markets directed by the newly formed United Nations. Free markets, they believed, would keep the peace, spur democracy, and bring people together economically and culturally.

The destruction of all the other industrialized economies allowed the United States to assert its liberally minded dominance over the world's economic affairs. In fact, more than a year before the end of World War II, world leaders from forty-four Allied nations, including the Soviet Union, gathered at Bretton Woods, New Hampshire, to discuss the economic future of a postwar world.

IN THEIR OWN WORDS

UN Secretary-General Kofi Annan

It has been said that arguing against globalization is like arguing against the laws of gravity, but that does not mean we should accept a law that allows only heavyweights to survive. On the contrary, we must make globalization an engine that lifts people out of hardship and misery, not a force that holds them down.

– From the opening address to the 53rd annual UN Department of Public Information NGO Conference, August 2000.

A meeting of world leaders at the United Nations Monetary and Financial Conference at the Mount Washington Hotel in Bretton Woods, New Hampshire, to discuss the establishment of new international economic systems following World War II.

Officially known as the United Nations Monetary and Financial Conference, the goal of the Bretton Woods meeting was to provide war-ravaged nations the financial help they needed to rebuild their shattered economies. Consequently, the conference created the International Monetary Fund (IMF) and the International Bank for Reconstruction and Development (IBRD), which is now part of the World Bank.

The guiding principle of the Bretton Woods Conference was the belief that free trade promotes international prosperity and peace. Roosevelt, along with many of those who attended Bretton Woods, believed that high **tariffs** and the **devaluation** of currencies—undertaken to help countries compete better against each other in trade—all contributed to the economic calamity that preceded World War II and led to the rise of Nazi Germany and Imperial Japan, the two main protagonists in the war.

One of the first acts of the IMF, therefore, was to establish a monetary system to stabilize exchange rates (rates at which one country's currency is valued against another's). Given the strength of the U.S. economy after the war, the IMF used the U.S. dollar as

THE WORLD BANK

The World Bank provides financial and technical assistance to developing countries in an effort to alleviate poverty and improve living standards. IBRD, which is part of the World Bank, provides loans to middle-income and creditworthy poor countries. The first loan, $250 million, was given to France in 1947 to rebuild its **infrastructure**.

The International Development Association (IDA) provides grants to poor countries. Together, the World Bank and the IDA try to help developing nations by providing low-interest loans, interest-free credit, and grants for education, health, infrastructure, communications, and many other purposes.

an exchange-rate standard, requiring signers to the IMF agreement to tie the value of their currency to the dollar, which in turn was tied to the value of gold; establishing a gold standard.

A Second System

As the United States took its seat as a military and economic superpower in the postwar world, a second economic and social system emerged stronger than ever—**communism**. Communism is a social and economic philosophy characterized by a classless society and the absence of private property.

The idea of a **capitalist**-run system of globalization dominated by the United States was repugnant to Joseph Stalin, the communist leader of the Soviet Union since the mid-1920s. Even before the war ended, Stalin had begun economically and politically dominating Eastern Europe. After the war, Stalin believed the new monetary system emerging from Bretton Woods put the United States in the driver's seat, a leadership role he was not willing to give up. In fact, the Soviet Union did not sign on to the Bretton Woods institutions.

In Stalin's view, and the view of other Soviet leaders, the Great Depression and World War II were symptoms of an inferior capitalist system. The disastrous economic conditions following the war made Germany and other nations a prime target for the communist system. In Germany alone, the war had destroyed 25 percent of all urban housing and caused the country's gross domestic product—the total value of goods and services produced by a country—to fall 70 percent.

Joseph Stalin, pictured here delivering the eulogy at the funeral of the supreme commander of the Soviet Union's Red Army, Mikhail V. Frunze, in November 1925.

The Marshall Plan was put to work in Germany in the postwar years, as symbolized by this worker in West Berlin.

> ### IN THEIR OWN WORDS
> #### U.S. Secretary of State George Marshall
> Our policy is directed not against any country or doctrine but against hunger, poverty, desperation, and chaos. Its purpose should be the revival of a working economy in the world so as to permit the emergence of . . . conditions in which free institutions can exist.
>
> – From a speech at Harvard University, June 5, 1947.

Marshall Plan

American policy makers feared that if the United States did not take a more active role in rebuilding Western Europe, the Soviets would control all of Europe. As Stalin slowly consolidated power over Poland, the Balkans, East Germany, and other Eastern European nations, U.S. secretary of state George Marshall unveiled an economic plan to rebuild Western Europe.

In March 1948, Congress passed the Economic Cooperation Act—the Marshall Plan—earmarking $12 billion to reconstruct Europe. The plan jumpstarted industrialization and stimulated the U.S. economy by establishing new overseas markets for American-made products. Eventually, sixteen nations participated in the Marshall Plan, receiving nearly $13 billion in aid and allowing their economies to grow quickly. Just as importantly, the Marshall Plan stopped the communists from expanding westward.

GATT

In addition to the Marshall Plan, the IMF, and the IBRD, the Western democracies also created the General Agreement on Tariffs and Trade (GATT), which would set international trade rules. The idea of GATT, established in 1947, was to treat every country fairly as their economies expanded.

At the heart of GATT was "most favored nation" status, or MFN. Under this designation, nations treated foreign businesses equally by eliminating barriers to foreign trade and reducing tariffs.

All of the institutions put in place after the war—GATT, the IMF, and the World Bank—opened foreign markets to investment, which helped a good portion of the world rebuild.

Communist Bloc

Still, Stalin was not going to sit idle while the West dominated world economic affairs. Under Stalin, the Soviet Union formed a coalition of nations, not always of the willing, that would become known as the Communist Bloc, or Eastern Bloc, to head off the apparent threat of an American-led global capitalist economy. The Soviet leader foresaw a world split into two markets—one communist, the other capitalist. He believed that the communist system would win out, as it promoted full industrialization.

To that end, Stalin in 1949 helped form the Council for Mutual Economic Assistance, which included such nations as the Soviet Union, Poland, Hungary, Romania, Czechoslovakia, and East Germany. The idea behind COMECON was to foster trade among its member states, while urging "specialization" in manufacturing. That would reduce "parallelism," or duplication of industrial production.

A very chilly Cold War had begun. Because each economic system needed to be safeguarded, the United States led the formation of the North Atlantic Treaty Organization (NATO), a military alliance between the United States and most of the Western democracies, while, in response, the Soviet Union and its satellite countries formed the Warsaw Pact.

14   TRADE, ECONOMIC LIFE, AND GLOBALIZATION

Text-Dependent Questions

1. What was the purpose of the Bretton Woods Conference?
2. How many countries participated in the Marshall Plan, and how much money were they granted all together?
3. How did the economic conditions after World War II help spur the Cold War?

Research Projects

1. Use the library and the Internet to research the Marshall Plan and its successes and failures. Use that information to write a persuasive essay as to whether the Marshall Plan should have been extended into Eastern Europe.
2. Print out a political line map of Europe and highlight with shading the way the countries in Europe were aligned in the 1950s as the Cold War took shape—using one shade for capitalist countries and another for the communist countries.

Educational Videos

Bretton Woods Agreement
Page 11
"The Bretton Woods Agreement is a famous international monetary agreement that came out of a meeting of the United Nations Monetary and Financial Conference held in Bretton Woods, New Hampshire, from July 1 to July 22, 1944."
Published online by Investopedia.
http://www.investopedia.com/video/play/bretton-woods-agreement/.

The Marshall Plan
Page 13
"This short video has footage of George Marshall testifying before Congress in January, 1948 about the Marshall Plan to rebuild Europe after World War II."
Published on YouTube by journalist and author Mark Lambers.
https://youtu.be/lUd2W6aMng4.

Celebrations in Algeria in 1962 when the country gained its independence from France.

WORDS TO UNDERSTAND

fledgling: young and unformed.

guerrillas: soldiers who are not part of a regular military unit, usually fighting to overthrow the government.

imperialism: political and economic domination of one country by another.

impoverished: poor and destitute.

CHAPTER 2

Spheres of Influence

At the end of World War II, the United States and Soviet Union had partitioned Europe into economic and political spheres of influence. But the world is much larger than Europe. The Soviets had set their sights on dominating Africa and Asia, and America had competing interests there.

Complicating matters for both nations was an independence movement that spread across those regions, one that was sanctioned by the newly established United Nations, which adopted the principle of self-determination at its founding in 1945. At the time, the British, French, Belgian, and Dutch empires were in a state of decline. Each found it difficult to maintain its colonies in Africa and Asia after the war. Some colonies achieved independence through peaceful negotiation. For example, Mahatma Gandhi led a long nonviolent campaign to free India from Great Britain, which granted it independence in 1947.

Others, however, pursued a more radical armed approach. Algeria secured its independence from France in 1962 after a lengthy war. Moreover, anticolonial movements took root in Vietnam, Angola, and in Latin America. As a result, ethnic and religious groups that had nothing in common and often mistrusted one another were thrown together to build new nations and economies. These differences often led to political instability and war.

Both Soviets and Americans eyed many of these **fledgling** nations as potential military and economic allies. For its part, the United States advocated for liberation movements, hoping to create new economic allies as its old colonial partners in Europe struggled to regain their economic footholds. The United States wanted to open up new countries to free markets, economic systems in which businesses operate without government controls, including fostering the development of raw-materials export businesses. From 1945 to 1980, private investment by the United States in developing countries increased dramatically, from $4 billion to $40 billion, while military aid totaled $200 billion.

The United States also tried to win hearts and minds. Teams of workers and volunteers fanned out across Latin America, Africa, and Asia, helping those living in **impoverished** areas. The Peace Corps, established in 1961, was an example of this. Volunteers built sewer systems, hospitals, schools, bridges, and other projects. The United States also provided banking assistance.

For its part, the Soviet Union hoped to entice these newly independent countries by highlighting its controlled economy and classless society. The Soviets wanted to dominate the Third World, as it would later be called, in order to spread the gospel of communism and eliminate capitalism. Soviet leader Nikita Khrushchev exclaimed that capitalism "goes hand in hand with the plunder of the oppressed country . . . and the preservation of backward socio-economic reform."

The Soviets also wanted to foster a social revolution, geared toward communism, while also exploiting the developing world's raw materials and using territory as sites for military bases.

In 1962, Peace Corps volunteers demonstrate to women in East Pakistan (now Bangladesh) the way a rice huller works. The device removes the outer husks, saving time in the processing of the grain for food.

Third World liberation leaders and **guerrillas** frequently and eagerly sought help from either the Soviets or the Americans. Often, these leaders played one side against the other. Moreover, each superpower supported brutal regimes.

Meeting at Bandung

Knowing they were caught in the middle, representatives from twenty-nine developing Middle Eastern, Asian, and African governments met in Bandung, Indonesia, in April 1955, to discuss the role their nations should play as it related to economics, development, and decolonization. The conference grew out of an increasing sense of isolation among the countries that did not choose sides with either the Soviet Union or the United States.

The driving idea behind the Bandung Conference was to formulate a set of principles that would guide each country in their relations with the "developed" world. Delegates talked about nonaggression, self-determination, and equality.

At the meeting, speaker upon speaker railed against colonialism and **imperialism** and cried out for the freedom of all subjugated peoples. Delegates vowed not to take sides in the escalating Cold War.

It was a groundbreaking meeting. Most of the states that attended, in the words of the *New York Times*, "might not even have been imagined a generation ago. There is hardly a state in the Bandung list whose representatives did not speak for peoples who have undergone profound and even revolutionary changes in political and social environment within a relatively short time." At the end of the conference, the delegates pledged to rely on themselves and not foreign aid.

> **VIEW FROM WASHINGTON**
>
> Watching from Washington, American officials viewed the Bandung Conference with grave suspicions. They feared the meeting would become a politically left-leaning attempt by the many countries, especially those in Africa and Asia, to side with the Soviet Union.
>
> Moreover, the United States was wedged in a political and diplomatic vice. While the United States wanted to show its support for decolonization, it still had to cooperate with Britain, France, and the Netherlands for their support in Europe to block Soviet aggression.

Neocolonialism

As the Cold War continued, the United States slowly became the dominant economic power in many of the emerging nations. This trend came to be known as neocolonialism. As an example, the U.S. government under the leadership of President Harry S. Truman began offering large sums of money to any government as a bulwark against communism.

Truman devised the doctrine as communist-led insurgents, or rebels, threatened Greece and Turkey. Truman argued that it was important to support free and independent countries in the face of Soviet totalitarian expansion. Truman said the security of the United States depended on such intervention.

IN THEIR OWN WORDS

President Harry S. Truman

I believe that it must be the policy of the United States to support free peoples who are resisting attempted subjugation by armed minorities or by outside pressures. I believe that we must assist free peoples to work out their own destinies in their own way. I believe that our help should be primarily through economic and financial aid, which is essential to economic stability and orderly political processes.

– From a speech before a joint session of the U.S. Congress, March 12, 1947.

The so-called Truman Doctrine allowed the United States to extend its sphere of influence and, in many instances, to place foreign governments under its control. The United States routinely interfered in domestic conflicts. It also backed regimes that wanted to do business with American companies even though it was not in the best interests of their citizens.

The Cold War became even more complicated when China fell to the communists in 1949. While the U.S.-backed nationalists retreated to the small island of Taiwan, Mao Zedong became the leader of the People's Republic of China. It was a devastating blow for the Western democracies. Nearly a quarter of the world's population was now under Communist control.

Helping to Unify Europe

As the 1950s began, much of Western Europe was fully on board with the liberal Western economic policies. In 1950, French foreign minister Robert Schuman proposed creating a European Coal and Steel Community (ECSC). Members of the ECSC, , established in 1952, which was established in 1952, included France, West Germany, Italy, Netherlands, Belgium, and Luxembourg, agreed to pool all coal and steel production in an attempt to make life better for millions.

The goal of the ECSC was to head off another great war by making France and Germany—historic rivals—economically dependent on one another. The ECSC also helped to create a more united Europe.

A Divided Germany

At the end of World War II, Germany was split into zones of occupation. The communist Soviet Union dominated East Germany, while the capitalist democracies of the United States, France, and Britain had influence over West Germany.

The outcome could not have been starker. West Germany saw a rapid economic recovery, in part because of its own internal political system and the outside help of the Economic Cooperation Administration, a U.S. agency that administered the Marshall Plan. Paul Hoffman, who ran the agency, suggested the formation of a united

Protests in Berlin and throughout East Germany about economic conditions in 1953 were met with Soviet tanks; pictured here is the scene in Leipzig on June 17.

INSIDE THE BOX

No one today gives the humble shipping container a second thought. Yet in the early days of the Cold War, shipping containers proved to be a valuable driver of globalization. When World War II ended, port cities offloaded cargo as they had for centuries. Longshoremen crawled into the holds of ships and unloaded every crate and box by hand. It was slow. It was expensive. Shipping containers, first introduced in 1956, changed all that.

The containers allowed goods to be uniformly packed and offloaded from a ship directly onto a truck or railcar. It saved time and money. More importantly, it increased trade.

Western European market that would eliminate custom and trade barriers, an idea that would be a seed for today's European Union.

For its part, communist East Germany stagnated during the early years of the Cold War. Economic conditions in East Germany were so bad in 1953 that 50,000 workers stood toe-to-toe with the Soviet Army in East Berlin in protest. Protests soon spread to the rest of East Germany, and to Poland, Hungary, and Czechoslovakia. All demanded economic reforms. In most cases, the Soviet military put down the revolts.

Text-Dependent Questions

1. Explain how competition between the Soviet Union and the United States affected the Third World.
2. What was the theory behind the Truman Doctrine?
3. Why did the United States view the Bandung Conference with suspicion?

Research Projects

1. Use the Internet and library to research which nations won their independence during the Cold War. Next, print out a political line map of Africa. Color in the nations that aligned themselves with the Soviet Union. Use another color to show the nations that aligned themselves with the United States.
2. Select one of the leaders discussed in the chapter—either Soviet leader Nikita Khrushchev or U.S. president Harry S. Truman—and write a brief biography of the leader, focusing on the early days of the person's political career and how that led to his leadership role.

Educational Videos

Mini Bio: Gandhi
Page 17
"Mahatma Gandhi was an international symbol for human rights whose personal dedication to nonviolent resistance inspired generations. Find out more about his life and work in this mini biography."
Published on YouTube by Biography.com.
https://youtu.be/ept8hwPQQNg.

President John F. Kennedy Announces the Executive Order to Form Peace Corps
Page 18
"March 1, 1961—President John F. Kennedy announces the formation of the Peace Corps at a press conference."
Published on YouTube by the Peace Corps.
https://youtu.be/7y2mZH1dVeA.

WORDS TO UNDERSTAND

dissonance: lack of consistency between two comparable ideas or actions.

fiscal: having to do with financial matters.

precursor: something that comes before, and hints at the arrival of, something else.

reams: a huge amount.

ABOVE: The encounter between U.S. vice president Richard Nixon and Soviet premier Nikita Khrushchev in the "Kitchen Debate."

CHAPTER 3

Consumer Societies Emerge in the West

As the Cold War began, so did a new era in consumerism. It started first in the United States and quickly spread throughout the noncommunist world. Consumerism, the belief that personal consumption of material goods is a sign of economic health and strength, encourages the acquisition of goods and increases choice for consumers. It also spurs competition among companies, which in turn brings down the price of products and services.

In the postwar world, the Western economies brimmed with new homes, cars, televisions, washing machines, toasters, and vacuum cleaners. For most people, buying such items, luxuries to many, was a new concept. Only a few short years before, people bought only the necessities because they could afford little else. The war's aftermath changed all that, at least in the United States. After fifteen years of depression and war, consumerism created prosperity, which created a strong economy.

Consumerism, Economic Growth, and the Cold War

It wasn't just pent-up demand that fueled economic growth. The Cold War helped to stir innovation. With the heightening of competition between the United States and the Soviet Union, economic resources were poured into research and development (R&D), primarily for defense systems, spurring an arms race that would have many offshoots into civilian commerce in noncommunist countries. The Internet itself, for instance, was the brainchild of the U.S. Defense Advanced Research Projects Agency (DARPA), established initially as ARPA in 1958.

As the noncommunist world prospered in the 1950s, the communists still believed their economic model ranked with that of Western countries. On July 24, 1959, U.S. vice president Richard Nixon and Soviet premier Nikita Khrushchev got into a heated argument about capitalism versus communism at a model kitchen set up for the American National Exhibition in Moscow, which followed an exhibit in New York City of Soviet culture earlier that year, in June. In hindsight, it was the perfect setting to underscore the economic **dissonance** between capitalism and communism.

IN THEIR OWN WORDS

Vice President Richard Nixon and Premier Nikita Khrushchev during the "Kitchen Debate"

Nixon: This house can be bought for $14,000, and most American [veterans from World War II] can buy a home in the bracket of $10,000 to $15,000. Let me give you an example that you can appreciate. Our steel workers as you know, are now on strike. But any steel worker could buy this house. They earn $3 an hour. This house costs about $100 a month to buy on a contract running 25 to 30 years.

Khrushchev: We have steel workers and peasants who can afford to spend $14,000 for a house. Your American houses are built to last only 20 years so builders could sell new houses at the end. We build firmly. We build for our children and grandchildren.

Nixon: American houses last for more than 20 years, but, even so, after 20 years, many Americans want a new house or a new kitchen. Their kitchen is obsolete by that time. . . . The American system is designed to take advantage of new inventions and new techniques.

Khrushchev: This theory does not hold water. Some things never get out of date—houses, for instance, and furniture, furnishings—perhaps—but not houses. . . .

— From the "Kitchen Debate" between U.S. vice president Richard Nixon and Soviet premier Nikita Khrushchev.

Advertising and Marketing

In a consumer-driven society, consumption is good, and consuming more is better. Nothing powers consumption more than advertising. As the 1950s ushered in a golden age of consumerism, it also created a revolution in advertising. Advertising was essential to a free market. It fueled consumerism, which created demand for products.

Leo Burnett knew about the power of advertising. Burnett was an advertising wizard who helped develop a concept called "branding." Burnett understood why people wanted certain things. Before Burnett came on the scene, most advertisements contained **reams** of information that educated consumers about a product. Burnett trashed that practice. He strove to "brand" the image of a product into the minds of consumers. Advertising icons such as the Marlboro Man, Tony the Tiger, the Jolly Green Giant, and the Pillsbury Doughboy were all Burnett's creations.

Advertisers were partly responsible for the upward mobility of the Western world. They wanted their products to be seen as technologically superior and to reflect optimism. To that end, American companies in 1950 spent $5.7 billion on advertising, double what they had spent in 1945.

Automobiles were among the most heavily advertised products. Cars now became extensions of their drivers. Cadillac was a master at creating an image of an automobile as a symbol of status—the best money could buy. Ford went down a different road. Yes, you could buy a big, expensive car, but why? You can have two Fords that "cost little more than one high-priced car."

Advertisers also targeted children and young adults. Magazines, soft drinks, records, and other products were specifically marketed to teen audiences. Advertisers didn't forget about mom.

McDonald's decried, "You Deserve a Break Today." The sale of hamburgers soared.

Advertising was just as important as the Marshall Plan and other **fiscal** policies in lifting Germany up after its devastation in World War II. Advertising drove West Germany's industrial engine and helped 60 million Germans spend their newfound wages.

They bought cars, refrigerators, televisions, and air conditioners. The European Common Market, a **precursor** to the European Union, supported advertising as a way to create markets that pushed production along. Advertising was also used as a weapon against communism, with messages that encouraged "Strength for the Free World," an adage promoted by the Marshall Plan.

The "Jolly Green Giant," long the logo of the well-known Green Giant frozen vegetable company developed by advertising pioneer Leo Burnett.

The Middle Class Emerges

The effects were astounding. The West German middle class grew in size and power. White-collar workers, the so-called *Beamter* civil-servant class, emerged as a major component of the West German economy, spending a large amount of their disposable income on consumer products.

Other programs, especially in the United States, also sparked a rise in the middle class. After the war, Congress passed the G.I. Bill to help returning U.S. veterans. The G.I. Bill paved the way for soldiers to go to college and provided loans for homes and businesses.

The "good life" was now attainable. From 1944 to 1950, new home construction in the United States skyrocketed from 114,000 to 1.7 million. Suburbs sprung up across the country. William Levitt started selling mass-produced homes on Long Island, creating the quintessential suburban enclave, Levittown. It was easy to buy in, as long as you were Caucasian: no down payment, no closing costs, and no hidden fees. All a veteran had to do was put down $100 as a deposit, which buyers would end up getting back.

The Volkswagen plant in Wolfsburg, just west of the border from East Germany, in 1960. The plant here was famed for its production of the iconic VW "Beetle," seen here in production. The automobile industry helped fuel consumerism and the rise of the middle class throughout Western Europe and the United States.

The logo of Bank of America, the first company to offer a credit card to consumers for general use.

A New Capitalism

Western governments were spending money, too, helping fuel the rise in consumerism. Defense spending and aid to other nations created a huge demand for American products and services. Old industries, including steel and car making, flourished alongside new industries such as electronics, aviation, plastics, and computers.

Japan's economy, which was nearly ruined by the country's defeat in the war, rebounded on the strength of consumer-driven manufacturing and the huge American market. The Japanese began by building cars and later consumer electronics.

What was happening in the Western world was a new kind of capitalism, one, in the words of historian David Halberstam, "driven by a ferocious consumerism, where the impulse was not so much about what people needed in their lives but what they needed to consume in order to keep up with their neighbors."

The rise in consumerism also brought about a rise in debt. Before the war, people balked at taking out loans and buying on time. That's because most people were doubtful of their economic future. That all changed after the war. People became optimistic. Although they fretted about nuclear annihilation—the Soviets exploded their first atomic bomb in 1949—most people felt good about the economy.

Banks and businesses helped them along. Banks upped the amount of time that a person could pay back a car loan from twenty-four to thirty-six months. In the late 1950s, the Bank of America issued the first general-purpose credit card. Household and personal debt began to climb.

The Economic Landscape Changes

In the 1970s, with the postwar boom in Western countries over twenty years old, a transformation was beginning. What is referred to as Fordism—the reliance on mass production of goods to fuel industrial growth—was losing its effect. As the postwar need for consumer products became satisfied, economies began to slow down, eventually reducing economic growth.

FORDISM

The term "Fordism" comes from the early twentieth-century innovations of Henry Ford and the Ford Motor Company. While it is a broad concept, it basically refers to Ford's mass-production model: the ability to manufacture many identical products cheaply and provide workers with wages that support the demand for those products.

At the same time Fordism was waning, the Bretton Woods monetary system, established by the IMF after World War II, began to unwind. Keeping currencies tied to the U.S. dollar was no longer viable, as the dollar came to be seen as more and more overvalued. In 1971, Richard Nixon, then U.S. president, temporarily suspended the dollar's link to gold, but in 1973 the delinking was made permanent.

By the 1980s, a wave of economic globalization took root and advances in information technology (IT) reshaped business and industry. In fact, the two trends were interdependent and grew stronger as the decades moved on. Computer and communications technologies helped to shrink the economic world by removing national barriers to trade and financing. Changes in manufacturing were pronounced as well. For instance, parts of one product could be made in different countries, assembled in another, and sold in still other countries and regions.

The Soviet Union and its satellite countries, with their heavy-handed state-run economies, couldn't adapt to new technological developments and economic globalization the way Western countries did. Where once communist and noncommunist countries might have been on similar paths of economic growth in the postwar world, the gap began to widen considerably.

Model T's coming off the Ford Motor Company assembly line in 1913.

Text-Dependent Questions

1. Explain how advertising can affect a country's economy.
2. What was the G.I. Bill?
3. How did consumerism and advertising affect West Germany's economy after the war?

Research Projects

1. Use the Internet and the library to research magazine or newspaper advertisements of the Cold War period. Print or copy the advertisements and create a montage that you can then share with your class. Study the advertisements with these questions in mind: What is the advertisement selling? Do the illustrations (or photos) and text make these effective advertisements? Discuss your opinions with your classmates.

2. Find a transcript online of the "Kitchen Debate" discussed in this chapter and analyze the exchange between Vice President Richard Nixon and Premier Nikita Khrushchev. Next, perform it in several pairs as a piece of reader's theater, with each pair of actors seeking to influence each other in different ways.

Soviet premiere Mikhail Gorbachev and U. S. president Ronald Reagan during the Moscow Summit in 1988. Gorbachev advocated policies of openness ("glosnost") and economic restructuring ("perestroika") that contributed to the collapse of the Soviet system.

WORDS TO UNDERSTAND

bipolar: characterized by opposite moods, viewpoints, or ideas.

e-commerce: business conducted on the Internet.

Pacific Rim: countries that border the Pacific Ocean.

reverberate: echo; be felt beyond the origin.

CHAPTER 4

Cold War Wanes, Free Trade Takes Hold

It was 1991, and the colossal military enterprise Leninetz was undergoing an extreme makeover in St. Petersburg, Russia. The firm once made radar units and other military equipment for the Soviet military. That was in the past. The Cold War was over. The Soviet government had collapsed, its brand of communism relegated to the history books.

For decades, Soviet officials had treated Leninetz well, but now its factories struggled to come to terms with communism's demise. It retooled and began making refrigerators, razor blades, and other products. It was new territory for the Russians, whose controlled economy dictated every aspect of production. In the end, the former Soviet Union had to look to the West for help.

By the late 1980s, communism had buckled under its own collective weight, unable to keep pace with the Western market economies. The change threw not only the former Soviet republics into chaos, but the rest of the former Communist Bloc as well. With the communist threat gone, the United States became the world's only economic and military superpower. Its liberal values of democracy, individualism, and free markets had triumphed.

The downfall of communism would **reverberate** across the globe. The postwar world had created economic stability in the Communist Bloc. Now, many former communist nations found themselves in unstable economic times as they transitioned from planned economies to free markets. Those countries that had not participated in the liberalized trade and open economies of globalization were now ready to reap its benefits—and its problems.

IN THEIR OWN WORDS

Anatoly Turchak, General Director of Leninetz

Unfortunately, the Soviet system didn't allow us to engage in much consumer-goods production. . . . We fell behind the West in making consumer goods, so we need a lot of Western help in this area to make our people's lives more comfortable.

– Reported in "Seeking to Give a New Life to a Dying Soviet Industry," *New York Times,* December 23, 1991.

Europe's Transition

Europe was ground zero for this transformation. After communism's fall in Eastern Europe, trade, travel, and communication across the continent became easier. Yet many European nations faced serious problems, such as an influx of immigrants, rising unemployment, and discrimination against foreigners.

In 1993, the European Common Market, formed during the Cold War to remove trade barriers, was renamed the European Union (EU). The EU opened up its membership to the former communist countries to help them deal with the shifting economic and political landscape. EU members began cooperating on various economic policies, including a transition in 2000 to a common currency, the euro. EU passports replaced the passports of individual nations.

At first, it was a tough road for many EU members. Prices skyrocketed. People lost their jobs. Slowly, however, things got better. Europe was no longer a **bipolar** continent, split between communism and capitalism. Liberalized economic policies were now taking root in many countries.

In Poland, for example, Western-style supermarkets brimming with new products replaced the dreary government-owned stores. Fast-food restaurants opened. Foreign investors built factories, hotels, and malls. A reunified Germany achieved amazing success, becoming Europe's richest nation and a world leader in iron, steel, and coal production.

The flag of the European Union, which continued the work of the European Common Market in breaking down trade barriers among the countries of Europe; the EU would also establish a common currency among its members in 2001.

Some countries, however, including Russia, faced difficult times adjusting to the new global order. In 1998, Russia narrowly avoided a financial collapse. High inflation devalued the ruble, Russia's currency.

Changes in Asia and China on the Rise

Asia's economy began experiencing tremendous highs. Japan was the ultimate success story, becoming a leader in car manufacturing. Japan exported 10,000 cars in 1961 and 1 million a decade later. Business was so good that in the 1980s, Japanese automakers built factories in the United States. By 2008, Toyota became the world's largest carmaker, a title it held for three years and reclaimed in 2012.

Japan's factories diversified and began making and exporting TVs, cell phones, computers, and other consumer electronics. Japan was successful, in part, because its government followed a policy known as protectionism, which limited foreign imports. Protectionism put foreign companies at a disadvantage. Nations, including the United States, could not sell as many products in Japan as they wanted.

China also benefited from this new era of globalization. When Mao Zedong ruled China, he and the communists controlled every aspect of Chinese life. Mao wanted to compete with the world's richest nations. He tried to transform life through his Great Leap Forward program, which from 1958 to 1961, attempted to boost the country's agricultural and industrial production. Mao's Great Leap was a failure.

After Mao's death in 1976, China began to move to a centrally planned economy that had aspects of capitalism. Under the leadership of Deng Xiaoping, who took the reins in 1978, China began to loosen the grip the government had over economic activity, even allowing farmers to sell their own products in the marketplace.

China's leader Deng Xiaoping (center), with his wife by his side, visits the Johnson Space Center in Houston, Texas, in 1979; Deng would lead China in gradually opening up its economy to market forces in the years that followed.

Downtown Seoul, South Korea, one of the "Asian Tigers," so-called due to their fast-paced economic growth and rapidly expanding trade.

The government would come to shut down many of its state-run factories. It gave foreign companies permission to access the Chinese market. By 2010, China had become the world's largest exporter of goods and the world's second largest economy, behind the United States. China's middle class grew. Yet, while wages increased, most workers did not earn as much as those in other countries.

Low wages allowed China to keep prices down, which allowed it to sell more products overseas. China's prosperity was a double-edged sword for its trading partners. Its inexpensive products made lives better for millions around the world. However, other countries had a hard time competing. They could not make products as inexpensively as the Chinese did.

China and Japan weren't the only Asian nations to prosper following the end of the Cold War. Taiwan, Hong Kong, Singapore, and South Korea were able to modernize and industrialize, which allowed their economies to grow. These nations were nicknamed the Asian Tigers because of their economic success.

At first, each economy focused on light manufacturing, creating and exporting products such as textiles. As their economies grew, factories began making electronics and, later, automobiles, specifically in South Korea. Low wages, long hours, and worker loyalty helped drive the success of the Asian Tigers.

A Brave New Digital World

Digital technology redefined globalization as the twentieth century waned. By the 1990s, the emergence of the Internet, cell phones, and other forms of digital of communication changed the way people received and shared information. Individuals could now instantly communicate with anyone anywhere and at any time. People had access to a storehouse of information from which they could grow their businesses.

Governments and companies used this technology to exchange data, research, and other types of information in real time. The digital revolution increased cooperation between nations and allowed many businesses to expand and generate greater profits. Companies started selling their wares over the World Wide Web. **E-commerce** contributed to economic growth, even in far-off places. Peruvian farmers, for example, began selling their products online, increasing profits for many.

Moreover, the digital revolution created new industries and new occupations. Steve Jobs, the cofounder of Apple who died in 2011 of pancreatic cancer, created a company that for a brief moment surpassed the oil giant ExxonMobil as the top corporation in terms of revenue in the United States. The innovation of Bill Gates and his Windows computer operating system changed the way all of us interact with computers. Other entrepreneurs created companies such as Amazon, eBay, Facebook, and Google, which are among the most profitable in the world.

Globalization in Developing Countries

In Uganda, groups of women travel the countryside selling clean-burning stoves, toiletries, and drugs that battle malaria. In India, women sign people up for a program that uses text messages to get a loan. In Argentina, one woman began selling her own line of clothes in one store in Buenos Aires in 2001. Today she has eighteen.

Such new business ventures in the developing world were just pipe dreams when the Cold War ended. By the twenty-first century, they had become more common. However, trying to

REGIONAL AND GLOBAL TRADE ORGANIZATIONS

Regional trade is promoted through treaties, which also help to resolve issues among trading partners. The North American Free Trade Agreement is one such arrangement. NAFTA, as it is called, eased restrictions in an effort to promote trade among the United States, Mexico, and Canada. The Asia-Pacific Economic Cooperation, another organization, was formed to promote trade among the nations of the **Pacific Rim**. The European Union is perhaps the largest regional trade group in the world.

The World Trade Organization is a global organization designed to enforce free trade in all regions of the world. Formed in 1995, it aims to keep the General Agreement on Tariffs and Trade, established after World War II, strong, and to ensure that trade flows between countries as smoothly as possible.

The signing of NAFTA, with the leaders of the three member countries overseeing the ceremony: in the back row, from left to right, Mexico's Carlos Salinas, the United States' George H. W. Bush, and Canada's Brian Mulroney.

CHAPTER 4

spur economic growth in the developing world has not been easy. While globalization has ramped up economic activity in other parts of the globe, many developing nations, especially in Africa, have yet to share in the bounty. This is mostly reflected in sub-Saharan Africa, where 2.6 billion people live on only $2 a day.

The economic and political conditions in these countries have hampered the flow of trade, migration, communication, technology, and capital. Some sub-Saharan countries are dependent on imports, while their only export industries revolve around the extraction of a few natural resources, which often causes environmental degradation. The entry of many developing countries into the global marketplace is further complicated by poverty, debt, and a lack of education.

On the other hand, globalization has provided thousands of jobs in other developing nations, including India. Improved communications technology, the removal of trade barriers, and low wages all have made it easier for companies to transfer manufacturing and service jobs. While critics say such practices are examples of rich nations exploiting poor countries, others say that growth in developing economies would not be possible by any other means in a globalizing world.

The Nairobi National Park, where giraffes and other animals of the African savanna roam, seen against the skyline of Nairobi, Kenya, a thriving and bustling metropolis.

Text-Dependent Questions

1. How was China able to grow its government-run economy, while other communist nations failed?

2. Name three ways digital technology has reshaped the global marketplace.

3. Why has globalization been mostly absent from sub-Saharan Africa?

Research Projects

1. Break off into groups of three or four and brainstorm ways that globalization has impacted your community. For example, did a local factory close and ship jobs overseas? How many foreign restaurants and car dealers are there in your town? Make a list of your examples.

2. Go to the parking lot of your school (or a shopping center or mall) and count the number of automobiles that are made in other countries. List and tally the number of cars from each country that you see. What can you conclude?

The Airbus, one of the mainstays of Air France's fleet, at Charles de Gaulle Airport outside of Paris. Air France, now united with the Dutch carrier KLM, was once owned by the French state; in 2004, the government sold its majority share to private companies.

WORDS TO UNDERSTAND

deficits: amounts by which expenses exceed income.

deregulated: removed rules and regulations to help free an industry or economy from government oversight and control.

dogma: rigid belief in a system of ideas and values.

inflation: increasing prices and/or wages and other costs of production.

outsourcing: purchasing goods or services from outside sources to handle activities typically done locally.

privatization: transferring certain government functions to private enterprises.

CHAPTER 5

Free Markets Rule

The transfer of British Rail from government to private hands in 1997, the selldown of the French government's share of Air France-KLM to less than a majority in 2004, and the **outsourcing** of the U.S. base Camp Anaconda in the Iraq War starting in 2003: all these developments are part of a broader economic policy that has dominated governments for more than thirty years—neoliberalism.

Neoliberalism is an economic philosophy in which governments remove rules and regulations from markets and industries to spur economic growth. **Privatization** is one aspect of neoliberalism.

The underlying goal of neoliberalism is to allow free markets to regulate and balance themselves, which, in theory, would open up economic opportunity. According to this theory, wealth will "trickle down" from the rich to the middle class and poor, creating jobs and pouring money into the economy.

Neoliberalism versus Keynesian Economics

The idea of neoliberalism was first articulated in the 1930s by British economists as a way to avoid the economic failures that caused the Great Depression. The economists did not believe humans could create systems to stop such economic upheavals from occurring again.

For nearly thirty years after World War II, neoliberalism was not a functioning public policy in any country, including the United States. It ran counter to Keynesian economic theory (named for economist John Maynard Keynes), which said government spending was the only way to stimulate the economy in times of slow economic growth.

Keynesian economics dominated the postwar era. At that time, government, business, and labor agreed that social and economic ruin often occurred when governments left the financial markets unchecked and unregulated. Only government, through its monetary and fiscal policies, could reduce inequality and provide its citizens with basic services.

John Maynard Keynes, on the right, with Harry Dexter White, assistant secretary of the treasury, at the inaugural meeting of the International Monetary Fund's board of directors in 1946.

By the 1970s, much had changed. Some aspects of neoliberalism began to creep into public policy decisions. In Britain, Prime Ministers Harold Wilson and James Callaghan cut government spending deeply to rein in inflation. In the United States, President Jimmy Carter **deregulated** the banking and airline industries.

Reaganomics and Thatcherism

Yet it wasn't until Margaret Thatcher became prime minister of Great Britain in 1979 and Ronald Reagan was elected president of the United States in 1980 that neoliberalism became **dogma**. Both leaders maintained that government was the source of most economic problems. It was inefficient, burdensome, and costly, they said. It stifled, not bolstered, economic growth.

Reagan's economic policies, referred to as "Reaganomics," slowly created a shift in the American economy away from the Keynesian model. "Only by reducing the growth of government can we increase the growth of the economy," Reagan said, distilling his vision of neoliberalism into fifteen words.

Reagan's policies had four major pillars: reduce government spending, reduce tax rates, reduce regulation, and control the growth of the money supply. Both leaders and their economic advisers believed that these policies would increase savings and investments, boost economic growth, allow budgets to be balanced, reduce **inflation** and interest rates, and create healthy financial markets.

VOODOO ECONOMICS

George H. W. Bush, who ran against Ronald Reagan for the Republican nomination for president in 1980, called Reagan's neoliberal economic policies "voodoo economics" and "economic madness." Bush lost the nomination to Reagan but became his vice president.

Washington Consensus

Neoliberalism soon spread around the world as countries pulled back from participating in the economy. Governments transferred many programs to private companies. They lifted trade barriers on imports and restrictions on foreign investment.

Ronald Reagan, president of the United States, and Margaret Thatcher, prime minister of Great Britain, in 1984. The two leaders helped to launch an era of economic neoliberalism in their respective countries.

POINT-BY-POINT

The following ten points were all part of the Washington Consensus, a neoliberal framework to spur economic growth, especially in the Third World:

- Lower government borrowing to avoid large fiscal deficits.
- Limit the spending of public money on programs such as education, health care, and infrastructure, and support the application of private investment in these areas.
- Broaden the tax base and cut tax rates.
- Set interest rates that are driven by the market.
- Make exchange rates competitive.
- Make trade easier.
- Increase foreign direct investment (FDI).
- Privatize certain government functions.
- Abolish rules that hinder business competition, except in the areas of safety, environment, and finance.
- Secure intellectual property rights.

Stimulating this radical change was a set of ten policies championed by the United States and instituted globally by several international institutions, including the World Bank and IMF, to guide developing or struggling economies to fiscal health. These policies were known as the "Washington Consensus." The goal of the Washington Consensus was to reduce the role of government in developing nations by encouraging them to lower spending, reform tax rates, and privatize government programs.

Failure

In the minds of many, the Washington Consensus and the entire philosophy of neoliberalism was an abject failure. Critics, such as former World Bank chief economist Joseph Stiglitz, argued that neoliberal philosophy did not help countries achieve long-term growth. In fact, free-market liberalization "may actually have had a perverse effect," he said. "All too often, the dogma of liberalization became an end in itself, not a means to a better financial system."

Stiglitz, who said governments should have a hand in guiding economic development, wasn't alone in his condemnation. Many said the idea that economic prosperity "trickles down" from the rich, creating wealth for those below, was simply wrong. Moreover, it was responsible for triggering various economic crises around the world, including those in Latin America in the 1990s.

Furthermore, the inequity between the wealthiest and everybody else grew substantially. That scenario played out in India during the early 2000s. Increased opportunity has led to a growing middle class there; however, the wealthiest 10 percent has steadily accumulated more riches. In 2000, they controlled just over 65 percent of India's wealth. By 2014, that number had climbed to 74 percent. In addition, tax rates had become regressive. In other words, the rich were subject to lower rates of taxation, while everyone else paid more.

Lunchtime at the headquarters of the technology company Infosys in 2003 in Bangalore; Infosys is one of the firms that has helped raise income levels in India.

The reduction of state spending, a cornerstone of neoliberalism, also led to austerity. Because tax revenue was low, governments on all levels were forced to cut budgets by slicing education, health care, and other "safety net" programs that helped the poor and marginalized.

In Great Britain, Margaret Thatcher decreased subsidies to nationalized industries. She also cut money for housing and local governments. As a result, inflation increased, private investment declined, and joblessness rose to around 12 percent. The English economy was so bad in 1981 that riots erupted across the country.

In the United States, Reagan's first budget cut $39 billion in social spending, gutting programs used by the poor, disabled, and elderly. He also engineered a 25 percent reduction in taxes over three years. As he cut the rest of the federal budget, Reagan increased defense spending, which created higher **deficits**. During the Reagan years, the wealthiest 10 percent increased their incomes by nearly 30 percent, while 90 percent lost income.

Protesting Neoliberalism

Many movements have sprung up in recent years to protest the impact of neoliberalism. In 1999, activists descended on Seattle to protest the World Trade Organization Ministerial Conference, which met to negotiate trade issues. Protesters surrounded the Washington State Convention and Trade Center and the hotels where WTO delegates were staying, and there were instances of vandalism and looting. It was estimated that the protesters numbered at least 40,000 people, including union members, environmentalists, and labor rights groups, among others.

Another grassroots effort against neoliberal policies is the Occupy Movement, which started out as Occupy Wall Street in 2011 but spread to other cities and other countries. Among other things, the movement staged protests to argue against corporate greed and economic inequality, spreading their slogan, "We are the 99%."

Protests at the WTO conference in Seattle, Washington, 1999.

Text-Dependent Questions
1. How does Keynesian economics differ from neoliberalism?
2. What was the Washington Consensus?
3. What was one grassroots movement protesting against neoliberal policies?

Research Projects
1. Create and perform a fictional reader's theater piece based on what you read in this chapter. The parts for the reader's theater can include: a narrator, a government official who believes in neoliberalism, a community activist for the poor, a union organizer, a corporate executive, and an unemployed worker.
2. Research one of the protest movements discussed in this chapter and write a brief report on its origins, purposes, and activities.

Educational Video
1982 Voodoo Economics
Page 43
A description used by George H. W. Bush about President Ronald Reagan's economic policies during their 1980 campaign for the Republican presidential nomination. Published on YouTube by NBC News Archives.
https://youtu.be/o8hnM6xNjeU.

WORDS TO UNDERSTAND

assets: things of lasting value, such as land and buildings, that are often used as investments to earn income.

exploit: use or extract resources for economic gain.

market value: amount for which an asset, such as a home or car, can be sold.

recession: slow-down in economic growth resulting in unemployment and lower business income.

repercussions: problems that result from a specific action.

vagaries: unpredictable behaviors or outcomes.

ABOVE: Individual investors in China's stock market were faced with steeply falling prices in 2015.

CHAPTER

6

Globalization in Today's World

For nearly a year beginning in June 2014, China's stock market was humming. It increased 150 percent as investors dived into the market, mostly with borrowed money. The stocks they bought were overvalued, but the momentum continued, as did the heavy buying. Finally, it all came crashing down in a shuddering collapse of the Chinese stock market in June 2015. Another plunge in August erased most of the gains investors had earlier made.

China's response to its economic problems was, in part, to weaken, or devalue, its currency. A weak currency would help China's exporters sell their goods more inexpensively abroad. The move had major implications for countries that traded with China. It made Chinese imports more expensive, which created trade deficits in many nations.

The devaluation of China's currency also signaled that its economy, the second largest in the world, was far weaker than people had thought. Companies pulled back on their business, fearing China would no longer be as strong as it once was. As the Chinese economic crisis played out, it underscored the **vagaries** of globalization. It exposed a frightening fact: that financial problems in one nation can have major **repercussions** around the world.

The global economy allows people and organizations to invest in companies across the world. It lessens the cost of basic consumer products and helps to raise workers in developing countries out of poverty. However, when an economic crisis strikes, it spreads like wildfire. Investors panic. Companies close. Banks go under. Nothing illustrated this better than the 2008 economic crisis that began in the United States and quickly engulfed the world.

The Great Recession

A **recession** is when a country's economy contracts, or shrinks, for two or more quarters. By the beginning of 2008, the United States was in a full-blown economic crisis. The recession began when the U.S. housing market collapsed. In the years before the recession, homebuyers, mortgage lenders, Wall Street financial firms, and insurers had pushed the prices of homes up by almost 10 percent a year.

By 2007, those prices were falling. Homeowners with adjustable-rate mortgages saw their monthly payments go up substantially, to the point where they could no longer afford the payments. Many had their homes foreclosed, or taken back by their lenders. Moreover, as housing prices fell, so did the equity in those homes—that is, the difference between the **market value** and the outstanding loans on their properties. People could no longer borrow against their homes to finance other **assets** or operating expenses.

The collapse of the housing market was accompanied by other economic problems, such as huge losses on highly risky, poorly regulated investments based on mortgages. Banks and other financial companies packaged together existing

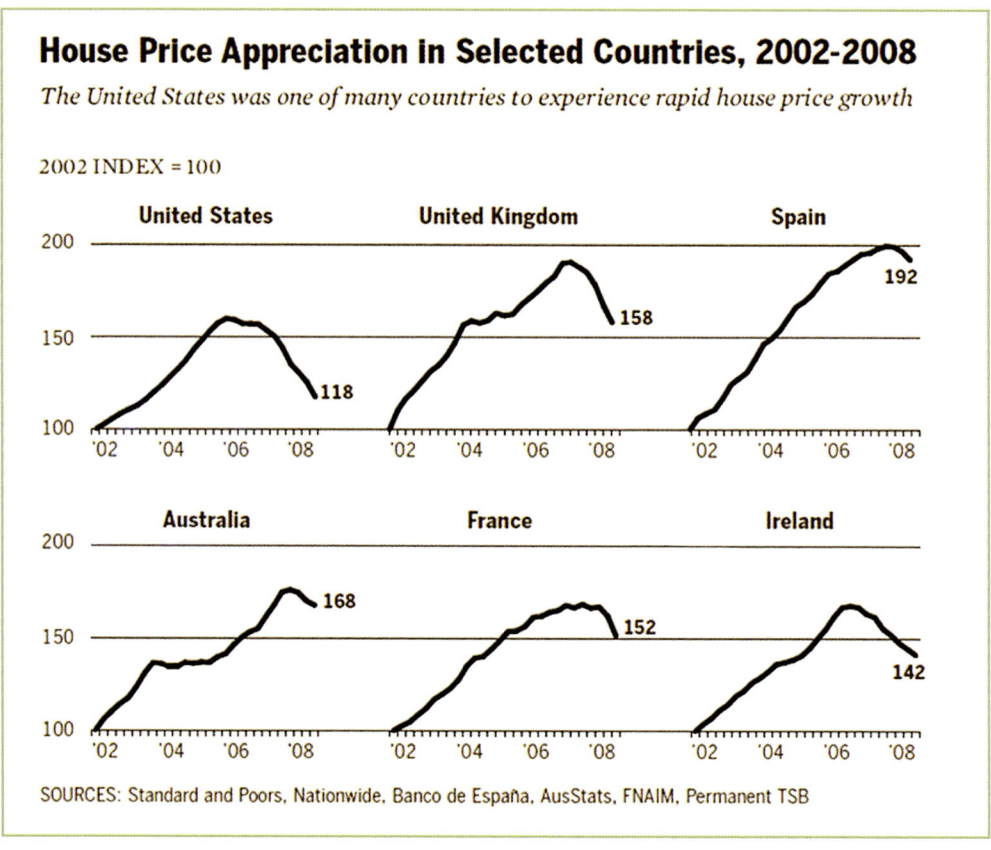

Presented in testimony before the U.S. Financial Crisis Inquiry Commission, this chart shows the rapid increase in the price of homes in key Western countries leading up to the financial crisis of 2007–2008.

Protest in Greece in 2013 against problems facing the middle class due to the Great Recession, as well as long-term internal economic issues.

mortgages and resold them to investors from across the country, as well as the world. As the underlying mortgages failed, so did these investments, which came to be called "toxic."

All this had a domino effect. Nearly 200 banks, mostly small and local, failed. The larger, more financially secure banks cut back on lending. Businesses found it harder and harder to borrow money to buy inventory or pay their workers. Many businesses failed. Stock prices dropped. Millions of people were laid off from their jobs. The auto industry, which relied on people's ability to borrow money, nearly collapsed. The government had to bail it out.

The recession spread quickly around the world. Europe, which has close financial ties to the United States, was hit the hardest, as was Japan. Many countries were forced to spend government money on stimulus packages to stem the economic downturn. Most succeeded, while others, such as Greece and Spain, found it difficult to recover.

Some Prosper

Globalization has been good for many people. It has increased global economic output and enriched many lives. Globalization was a factor in lifting 1 billion people

ECONOMIC CONTAGION

The spread of economic problems across borders, such as what happened in 2008, is nothing new. During the 1980s and 1990s, many countries were on the verge of economic meltdowns. In 1997, a financial crisis reverberated through Asia, raising fears of a worldwide economic collapse. The crisis began in Thailand and then spread through much of East Asia over a series of currency devaluations. The crisis was somewhat checked when the IMF and World Bank intervened. Because of the so-called Asian Contagion, the economies of the United States and Europe slumped.

out of poverty—defined as people living on $1.25 or less a day—between 1990 and 2010.

Globalization has also allowed people from different cultures to intermingle and share their culture. People in the United States, for example, read Japanese comic books and listen to music from the Caribbean. Movies from India are hugely popular in Great Britain. In China, children used to dress in drab military clothes like their leader Mao. Now, teens sport Western-style fashions.

Although Japan has had various economic problems over the years, globalization has helped make it the world's third-largest manufacturing nation. China's rapid rise in economic prosperity, despite recent bumps and slowdowns in 2015, would not have been possible in isolation. Open markets and free trade allowed Brazil to expand the middle class, reduce poverty, and become Latin America's largest economy.

Others Struggle

While many countries and regions prosper, problems exist in both the industrial and developing worlds. Germany's economy blossomed greatly because of globalization. Yet over the years, its population has been aging and its birth rate has been declining, leading to a glut in jobs as people retire.

Germany has struggled to fill those jobs. To solve the problem, the government has undertaken many steps, including opening its doors to more immigrants from Eastern Europe. Many Germans became upset at the influx of immigrants. They feared the foreigners would take away jobs from natives and drive wages down.

Germany is not the only country that has a love-hate relationship with economic globalization. South Korea's rapid industrialization forced many people, especially the elderly, to live in urban slums as thousands moved from the countryside in search of work. In South America, the Amazon rain forest is under attack, as international companies **exploit** its natural resources, such as oil and gold.

In the United States, many companies have moved factories overseas. By moving to less economically developed countries, these companies are allowed to pay workers less in wages. In many instances, laws that protect the environment and worker safety are lax, which also lowers costs. Because of such outsourcing, a company can make a less expensive product and sell it at a lower cost, which increases profits. While these savings are often passed on to the consumer in reduced prices, the true cost in terms

A McDonald's in Dukhan, Qatar, in the Middle East.

of nonliving wages and the environment needs to be paid at some point—by governments that provide safety nets for the poor and by future generations who will eventually pay the cost of environmental degradation.

Back to Galesburg

Globalization can have a devastating impact on a community. No one knows this better than those living in Galesburg. When Maytag announced it was moving to Mexico, the local machinists' union and others forlornly fought the shutdown.

Five percent of the region's workforce lost jobs. The ripple effects created a tsunami of hardship. Restaurants where Maytag workers once ate were closed. Local businesses that supplied the factory with equipment had to lay off workers. The city itself saw a loss in tax

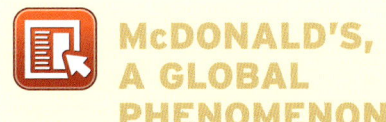

McDONALD'S, A GLOBAL PHENOMENON

Perhaps no one company symbolizes the transformative power of globalization more than McDonald's. In 1955, Ray Kroc opened his first fast-food store near Chicago. Today the chain has some 36,000 stores in 120 countries. And McDonald's has adapted to local customs. In India, you can get curried vegetables at the Golden Arches, and in Germany, bratwurst is on the menu.

CHAPTER 6   53

The rail yard in Galesburg, Illinois, still an active hub transporting domestic and international products across the United States.

revenue. According to a Western Illinois University study, the region lost 4,166 jobs. Most of the old factory is now gone.

Perhaps not all is lost, though. If you look at the rail yard in Galesburg, you will see that it teems with Asian products—all waiting to be sent to American stores. Nearby is a slaughterhouse where pigs are shipped around the globe. At nearby Knox College, 10 percent of students come from foreign lands.

It's possible that globalization is starting to reverse the city's decline and deliver on new promises.

Text-Dependent Questions

1. How many McDonald's are there across the world, and in how many countries does the fast-food chain exist?
2. How many Japanese today live in poverty?
3. What were the side effects of South Korea's rapid industrialization?

Research Projects

1. Use the Internet and library to research how one country's economic problems had a domino effect on other countries. Greece and Thailand are examples. When you've completed your research, create a timeline that illustrates the problem.
2. Look on the Internet for maps of McDonald's restaurants across the world. Select one of the locations outside your home country and research what that country's cuisine is like and how it might have affected the menu at McDonald's. Write a brief report of your findings.

Timeline

1944	Allied nations meet at Bretton Woods, New Hampshire, to establish the economic structure of the postwar world, resulting in the International Monetary Fund (IMF) and International Bank for Reconstruction and Development (IBRD), now part of the World Bank.
1945	By the end of World War II, more than 60 million people are killed and the economies of Europe and much of Asia are destroyed.
	At the United Nations founding, it adopts the principle of self-determination to help colonies of European empires move toward independence.
1947	The IBRD provides its first loan, $250 million, to France to help it rebuild its infrastructure.
	The General Agreement on Tariffs and Trade (GATT) is established to set postwar international trade rules.
	India gains its independence from Britain after a long nonviolent campaign led by Mahatma Gandhi.
	U.S. president Harry S. Truman Doctrine articulates the "Truman Doctrine," which promotes U.S. influence across the globe in order to "contain" Soviet expansion; the Cold War begins.
1948	The United States launches the Marshall Plan to help rebuild Europe; Stalin disallows the participation of the Soviet Union and its allies.
1949	In an escalation of the Cold War with the United States and its Western allies, the Soviet Union forms the Council for Mutual Economic Assistance to foster trade within the Communist Bloc.
	The Cold War becomes more complicated when China falls to the communists in the country's long civil war.
1950	The middle class grows rapidly in the United States, West Germany, and other Western countries following the end of World War II; new home construction in the United States skyrockets from 114,000 to 1.7 million.
	American companies spend $5.7 billion on advertising, double what they had spent in 1945.
1951	The European Coal and Steel Community (ECSC) is established to pool coal and steel production, with the goal of creating a more united Europe.
1953	Protests in Berlin and throughout East Germany about economic conditions are put down by Soviet tanks.

1955	Representatives from developing countries meet in Bandung, Indonesia, to support each other in maintaining neutrality in the Cold War.
	Ray Kroc opens his first fast-food store near Chicago; fifty years later, McDonald's will have some 36,000 stores in 120 countries.
1956	Shipping containers are introduced, allowing goods to be packed and shipped easily and greatly increasing trade on the open seas.
1958	The U.S. Defense Advanced Research Projects Agency, (DARPA, initially ARPA) is established in response to the Soviet launch of Sputnik; it would launch a prototype of the Internet in 1969.
	The Bank of America issues the first general-purpose credit card.
1959	In the "Kitchen Debates," U.S. vice president Richard Nixon and Soviet premier Nikita Khrushchev debate the merits of capitalism versus communism at the American National Exhibition in Moscow.
1961	The United States establishes the Peace Corps to help poor nations in the developing world and to help promote democracy in those regions.
1962	Algeria secures its independence from France after a lengthy war.
1971	Richard Nixon, then U.S. president, temporarily suspends the gold standard (the value of the U.S. dollar's link to gold); in 1973, the delinking is made permanent.
	Japan exports 1 million cars, compared to 10,000 a decade earlier.
1976	After Mao's death, China begins to move to a centrally planned economy, with aspects of capitalism, under the leadership of Deng Xiaoping.
1979	Margaret Thatcher becomes prime minister of Great Britain; Ronald Reagan is elected U.S. president the next year; under them, neoliberal policies flourish, including reducing government spending and deregulation of business.
1980	Since the end of World War II, private investment by the United States in developing countries increases from $4 billion to $40 billion, while military aid totals $200 billion.
1980s	Japanese automakers build factories in the United States.
1989	Soviet influence and control over the countries of Eastern Europe collapse; the Berlin Wall falls.
	The term "Washington Consensus" is coined to indicate a ten-point neoliberal framework to cure ailing economies and spur economic growth, especially in the Third World.
1990s	The emergence of the Internet, cell phones, and other forms of digital communication launch a revolution in social, business, and economic life.
1990s	Economic crisis debilitates many countries in Latin America, caused, according to some critics, by neoliberal policies.

Timeline (continued)

1991	The Soviet Union dissolves into separate republics, with Russia the largest and most powerful; the Cold War ends.
1992	The North American Free Trade Area (NAFTA) is signed to strengthen trade among Mexico, the United States, and Canada.
1993	The European Common Market, formed during the Cold War, is renamed the European Union (EU); it opens up membership to former communist countries to help them deal with post–Cold War economic challenges.
1995	The World Trade Organization (WTO) is established, aiming to strengthen the free trade principles of the General Agreement on Tariffs and Trade (GATT).
1997	The British government transfers its ownership of British Rail to private hands.
	A financial crisis reverberates through Asia, having started in Thailand, raising fears of a worldwide economic slowdown.
1998	Russia narrowly avoids a financial collapse, and high inflation forces a devaluation of Russia's currency.
1999	Activists descend on Seattle, Washington, to protest the WTO Ministerial Conference, which meets to negotiate free trade arrangements.
2000	Members of the EU adopt a common currency, the euro; EU passports replace those of individual nations.
2003	The United States outsources the management of Camp Anaconda, its army base in Iraq.
2004	The French government sells down its majority share of Air France-KLM, leaving it under private ownership.
2008	Japan automaker Toyota becomes the world's biggest carmaker, a title it holds for three years and then reclaims in 2012.
	A full-blown economic crisis in the United States, rooted in the collapse of the housing market, spreads across the world; the downturn comes to be called the "Great Recession."
2010	China becomes the world's largest exporter of goods and the world's second-largest economy, behind the United States, with a growing middle class.
	Over the past decade, 1 billion people are lifted out of poverty worldwide, with increased economic globalization taking some of the credit.
2014	Income inequality climbs in India, with the wealthiest 10 percent controlling 74 percent of the country's wealth, compared to 65 percent in 2000.
2015–2016	China's stock market plunges, sending concerns about a worldwide slowdown across the country and the world.

Further Research

BOOKS

Andrews, David. *Businesses without Borders: Globalization* (The Global Marketplace). Portsmouth, NH: Heinemann. 2010.

Jaffe, Eugene D. *Globalization and Development*. New York: Chelsea House. 2006.

LaBella, Laura. *How Globalization Works*. New York: Rosen Publishing Group. 2009.

Merino, Noel. *Globalization: Introducing Issues with Opposing Viewpoints*. Boston: Greenhaven Press. 2009.

ONLINE

BBC News: "Global Recession Timeline": http://news.bbc.co.uk/2/hi/business/8242825.stm.

University of Pennsylvania, College of Arts and Sciences: "A Quick Guide to the World History of Globalization": http://www.sas.upenn.edu/~dludden/global1.htm#PartI.

Yale Global Online: "The History of Globalization": http://yaleglobal.yale.edu/about/history.jsp.

NOTE TO EDUCATORS: This book contains both imperial and metric measurements as well as references to global practices and trends in an effort to encourage the student to gain a worldly perspective. We, as publishers, feel it's our role to give young adults the tools they need to thrive in a global society.

Index

Italicized page numbers refer to illustrations

A

advertising 26–27, *27,* 27–28
Africa 17–19, 38, *38*
Air France *40,* 41
Algeria *16,* 17
American National Exhibition (Moscow, 1959) 25–26
Angola 17
Annan, Kofi *10*
Apple Inc. 9, 37
Argentina 9, 37
arms race 25
Asia 10, 18–19, 35–36, *36,* 51–52. *See also* China
Asian Tigers 36
Asia-Pacific Economic Cooperation 37
atomic bomb 29
automobile production 26, *28,* 29, *30*
aviation and airline industry 29, 40, 42

B

Bandung Conference (1955) 19
Bangladesh (East Pakistan) *18*
Bank of America 29
banks *29,* 42–44, 50–51
Belgium 17, 20
Berlin 21, *21*
Brazil 52
Bretton Woods conference 10–12, *11,* 30
Britain 17, 19–20, 42–45
Burnett, Leo 26–27
Bush, George H. W. 37

C

Callaghan, James 42
Canada 37
capitalism 12, 14, 18, 20–21, 25–26, 29–30, 34–37
Carter, Jimmy 42
China 9; communist rule of 20; and globalization 9, *35,* 35–36, 52; stock market collapse (2015) *48,* 49
Cold War 14, 19–20, 25
colonialism and neocolonialism 17, 19–20
communism 12–14, *14,* 17–21, 25–26, 33–36
communist bloc (Eastern Bloc) 14, *14,* 33
computer technology 29–30, 36–37, *45*

consumerism 25–29, 51
Council for Mutual Economic Assistance (COMECON) 14
currency and monetary system 11–12, 30, 34, 44, 49, 52
Czechoslovakia 14, 21

D

Defense Advanced Research Projects Agency (DARPA) 25
defense spending 25, 29, 45
Deng Xiaoping *35, 35*
developing nations 10, 12, 17–20, 37–38, *38,* 44
dollar 30. *See also* currency and monetary system

E

Eastern Europe 12–13, 21
East Germany 13–14, 20–21, *21*. *See also* Germany
East Pakistan (Bangladesh) *18*
E-commerce 37
Economic Cooperation Act (Marshall Plan, 1948) *13,* 13–14, 20, 27
economic recession (2008) 49–52, *50–51*
education 28, 45
electronics industry 29
environmentalism 46, 52–53
Euro 34. *See also* currency
Europe: and 2008 recession 51; economic unification of 20, 22, 27, *28,* 34; and fall of communism *34,* 34–35; political spheres of influence in 17–19; postwar economies 10, 13–14
European Coal and Steel Community (ECSC) 20
European Common Market 27, 34
European Union (EU) 27, 34, *34*
ExxonMobil 37

F

Ford, Henry 26, 30
Fordism 29–30
Ford Motor Company 30, *30*
foreign investment 43–44
Foxconn Technology Group 9
France 12, *16,* 17, 19–20, *40,* 41
free markets 41, 44. *See also* capitalism
free trade 10–11, 37
Frunze, Mikhail V. *12*

G

Galesburg, Illinois 9, 53, *54*
Gandhi, Mahatma 17, 19
Gates, Bill 37
General Agreement on Tariffs and Trade (GATT) 14, 37
Germany: and globalization 52–53; postwar economy of 11–14, *13*, *27*, *28*; postwar occupation of 20–22, *21*; unification and economic growth 34
G.I. Bill 28
glasnost (openness) 32
globalization 9–10, 14, *21*, 30, 36–38, 49–54, *53–54*
gold standard 30
Gorbachev, Mikhail *32*
Great Britain. *See* Britain
Great Depression 12
Great Recession (2008) 49–52, *50–51*
Greece 19, 51, *51*, 54

H

Halberstam, David 29
health care 44–45
Hoffman, Paul 20
Hong Kong 36. *See also* China
housing and housing market 12, 28, 45, 50–51
Hungary 14, 21

I

immigration 34, 52
independence movements 17
India 17, 37–38, 44, *45*, 53
industrialization 10, 13–14, 29–30, 33, 36, 40, 51–52
inflation 43
Infosys Limited *45*
intellectual property rights 44
interest rates 43–44
International Bank for Re-construction and Development (IBRD) 11–12, 14
International Monetary Fund (IMF) 11–12, 14, 30, *42*, 44, 52
international trade 11, 14, *22*, 34, *36*, 38, 43–44, 49, *54*
Internet 36–37
Italy 20

J

Japan 11, 29, 35–36, 51–52, 54
jobs 9–10, 34, 38, 41, 45–46, 51–54
Jobs, Steve 37
Jolly Green Giant *27*

K

Kenya *38*
Keynes, John Maynard 41, *42*
Keynesian economic theory 41–42
Khrushchev, Nikita 18–19, *24*, 25–26
Kirchner, Néstor 9
Korea 36, *36*, 52, 54
Kroc, Ray 53

L

labor unions 46, 53
Latin America 17–19, 44, 52
Leninetz Company 33
Levitt, William 28
Levittown 28
Luxembourg 20

M

manufacturing 9, 14, 26, *28*, 29–30, *30*, 35–38, 52. *See also* industrialization
Mao Zedong 20, 35
Marshall, George 13, *13*
Marshall Plan *13*, 13–14, 20, 27
Maytag Corporation *8*, 9, 53
McDonald's 27, 53, *53*, 54
Mexico 9, 37, 53
middle class 9–10, 28, *28*, 36, 41, 44, *51*, 52
Middle East 19, *53*
military interests 12, 14, 17–18, 22, 25, 29, 33, 45
monetary system 11–12, 30, 34, 43–44, 49, 52
Moscow Summit (1988) *32*
most favored nation status 14
Mulroney, Brian 37

N

NAFTA (North American Free Trade Agreement) 37, *37*
nationalization 45
Nazis 11
neocolonialism and colonialism 17, 19–20
neoliberalism 41–46, *46*
Netherlands 17, 19–20
New York Times 19
Nixon, Richard *24*, 25–26, 30
North Atlantic Treaty Organization (NATO) 14

O

Obama, Barack 9
Occupy Wall Street 46
outsourcing 52–53. *See also* manufacturing

Index (continued)

P

Pacific Rim 37
Peace Corps *18,* 19
People's Republic of China 20. *See also* China
perestroika (economic restructuring) 32
Poland 13–14, 21, 34
postwar economy 11–12, *13,* 13–14, 20, 27, 41
privatization 40–41, 43–44
protectionism 35

R

Reagan, Ronald *32,* 42–43, *43,* 45
Reaganomics 42–43, 45
Romania 14
Roosevelt, Franklin 10–11
Russia 35. *See also* Soviet Union

S

Salinas, Carlos 37
Schuman, Robert 20
"Seeking to Give a New Life to a Dying Soviet Industry" *(New York Times)* 33
Singapore 36
social safety net programs 45, 53
South America. *See* Latin America
South Korea 36, *36,* 52, 54
Soviet Union: and arms race and Cold War 25, 29, *32;* collapse of 33; and developing countries 17–18; Eastern Europe influence 12, 14, 17, 21–22, *21,* 33; and globalization 30; and postwar economy 10
Spain 51
Stalin, Joseph 12, *12,* 14
steel industry 29
Stiglitz, Joseph 44

T

Taiwan 20, 36
tariffs 11, 14. *See also* international trade
taxes 43–45
technology industry 9, 29–30, *45*
Thailand 52
Thatcher, Margaret 42–45, *43,* 45
Thatcherism 42–43
Third World nations 18–19, 44. *See also* developing nations
trade barriers 14, 34, 38, 43, 49. *See also* international trade

"trickle down" theory 41, 44
Truman, Harry S. 10, 19–20, *20*
Truman Doctrine 20
Turchak, Anatoly 33
Turkey 19

U

Uganda 37
unemployment. *See* jobs
United Nations 10–12, *11,* 14, 17
United Nations Department of Public Information NGO Conference (2000) 10
United Nations Monetary and Financial Conference (Bretton Woods) 10–12, *11,* 30
United States: and developing countries 17–20; economic crisis and recession (2008) 49–52, *50;* and globalization 8–9, 29–30, 37, 52–53; and neoliberalism 41–42, 46; postwar economic and military influence 10, 12–14, 20, 25, 29; and Reaganomics 42–45
U.S. Financial Crisis Inquiry Commission 50

V

Vietnam 17
Volkswagen *28*

W

wages and working conditions 30, 36, 38, 40, 52–53
Warsaw Pact 14
Washington Consensus 43–44
West Germany: advertising and economic growth 27; and European Coal and Steel Community (ECSC) 20; growth of middle class 28; influence of U.S., France, and Britain 20; rapid economic recovery after World War II 20
White, Harry Dexter *42*
Wilson, Harold 42
World Bank 12, 14, 44, 52
World Trade Organization 37, *46*
World Trade Organization Ministerial Conference (Seattle, 1999) *46*
World War II 10, 12–14, 27
World Wide Web 36–37

Photo Credits

Page number	Page location	Archive/Photographer
8	Top	Flickr/David Wilson
10	Bottom	Wikimedia Commons/US Mission in Geneva
11	Top	Library of Congress
12	Bottom	Wikimedia Commons /Radetsky
13	Top	Wikimedia Commons /National Archives and Records Administration
13	Middle	Wikimedia Commons /Dutch National Archives
14	Bottom	Wikimedia Commons/Mosedschurte
16	Top	Wikimedia Commons /Asm ub
18	Bottom	Peace Corps Media Library
20	Bottom	Library of Congress
21	Full page	Wikimedia Commons /German Federal Archives
22	Bottom	Wikimedia Commons/Captain Albert E. Theberge, NOAA Corps
24	Top	Wikimedia Commons/O'Halloran, Thomas J.
27	Bottom	Flickr/Amy Meredith
28	Bottom	Flickr/Roger W
29	Top	Flickr/Topher
30	Bottom	Wikimedia Commons/Ford Company
32	Top	Wikimedia Commons /Ronald Reagan Presidential Library
34	Bottom	Wikimedia Commons/MPD01605
35	Top	Wikimedia Commons/NASA
36	Top	Shutterstock/Panya K
37	Bottom	Wikimedia Commons/David Valdez
38	Bottom	Shutterstock/John Wollwerth
40	Top	Wikimedia Commons/Captainm
42	Top	Wikimedia Commons/International Monetary Fund
43	Bottom	Wikimedia Commons/White House Photographic Office
45	Top	Wikimedia Commons/Zondor
46	Bottom	Wikimedia Commons/Jnarrin
48	Top	iStock/FangXiaNuo
50	Bottom	Wikimedia Commons/Financial Crisis Inquiry Commission
51	Top	Wikimedia Commons/Cogiati
53	Top	Wikimedia Commons/Vincent van Zeijst
54	Top	Wikimedia Commons/David Wilson
Cover	Top	Wikimedia Commons/National Archives and Records Administration
Cover	Left	Shutterstock/Dmitry Kalinovsky
Cover	Right	Wikimedia Commons/Ph0kin

About the Author and Advisor

Series Advisor

Ruud van Dijk teaches the history of international relations at the University of Amsterdam, the Netherlands. He studied history at Amsterdam, the University of Kansas, and Ohio University, where he obtained his Ph.D. in 1999. He has also taught at Carnegie Mellon University, Dickinson College, and the University of Wisconsin-Milwaukee, where he also served as editor at the Center for 21st Century Studies. He has published on the East-West conflict over Germany during the Cold War, the controversies over nuclear weapons in the 1970s and 1980s, and on the history of globalization. He is the senior editor of the *Encyclopedia of the Cold War* (2008) produced with MTM Publishing and published by Routledge.

Author

John Perritano is an award-winning journalist, writer, and editor from Southbury, Connecticut, who has written numerous articles and books on a variety of subjects including history, politics, and culture for such publishers as Mason Crest, National Geographic, Scholastic, and *Time/Life*. His articles have appeared on Discovery.com, Popular Mechanics.com, and other magazines and websites. He holds a master's degree in American History from Western Connecticut State University.